AuthorHouse™
1663 Liberty Drive
Bloomington, IN 47403
www.authorhouse.com
Phone: 1-800-839-8640

First published by AuthorHouse 8/10/10

ISBN: 978-1-4520-6670-7 (sc)

Library of Congress Control Number: 2010911876

Printed in the United States of America

This book is printed on acid-free paper.

authorHOUSE®

Cottage In The Park... The Series©

The Squirrel Who Almost Stole Halloween

Written by Debbie Rankin
Illustrated by Kelly McKernan

www.cottageinthepark.com

About The Squirrel Who Almost Stole Halloween

It is October 31st, the year is 2000 and the neighborhood is decorated for Halloween. It is one of our favorite nights at the Cottage In The Park because it is always filled with fun and adventure!

Wink, the official Halloween greeter at the front door of the Cottage, had an experience two days before this night of tricks or treats; an experience that involved a very mischievous Squirrel.

After 10 years Wink still remembers every moment of those two days in October and finally she is ready to tell everyone exactly what happened when a Squirrel named Gabby almost stole Halloween.

And, every bit of it is true.

Thank you for joining Cottage In The Park…The Series© and the latest adventure, *The Squirrel Who Almost Stole Halloween.*

Enjoy!

Debbie Rankin, Author
Kelly McKernan, Illustrator

Cottage In The Park Dedication and Acknowledgements

Dedication

"The Squirrel Who Almost Stole Halloween" is dedicated to my husband Ed.
We were blessed the day we found each other.
I love you.

Acknowledgments

Thanks, Wes Lowrance, for introducing me to Kelly McKernan, our magical illustrator.

Thank you, Kelly, for your softness, clarity and artistic talent. Your illustrations blend so well with the story, reflecting the emotions of Wink and the mischievous yet innocent personality of Gabby. And the hat remains strong throughout in this latest adventure from the Cottage In The Park…The Series.©

Thank you, Kay Borden for designing and caring for www.cottageinthepark.com. Thank you too for your camera work at the various events for Butch The Blue Jay. Now it is time to add to the fun with the pictures you will capture from the gatherings for *The Squirrel Who Almost Stole Halloween*.

And many many thanks for all of the support I have received from Ed, friends and people I have met through this series. Reading these fun stories that are straight from my heart and talking with so many people who love the fun world of our animal friends is inspiring. I hope The Cottage Series will inspire others to share their experiences with nature.

It is October 31st and the neighborhood is decorated for Halloween. It is one of our favorite nights at the Cottage In The Park, always filled with fun and adventure!

My name is Wink

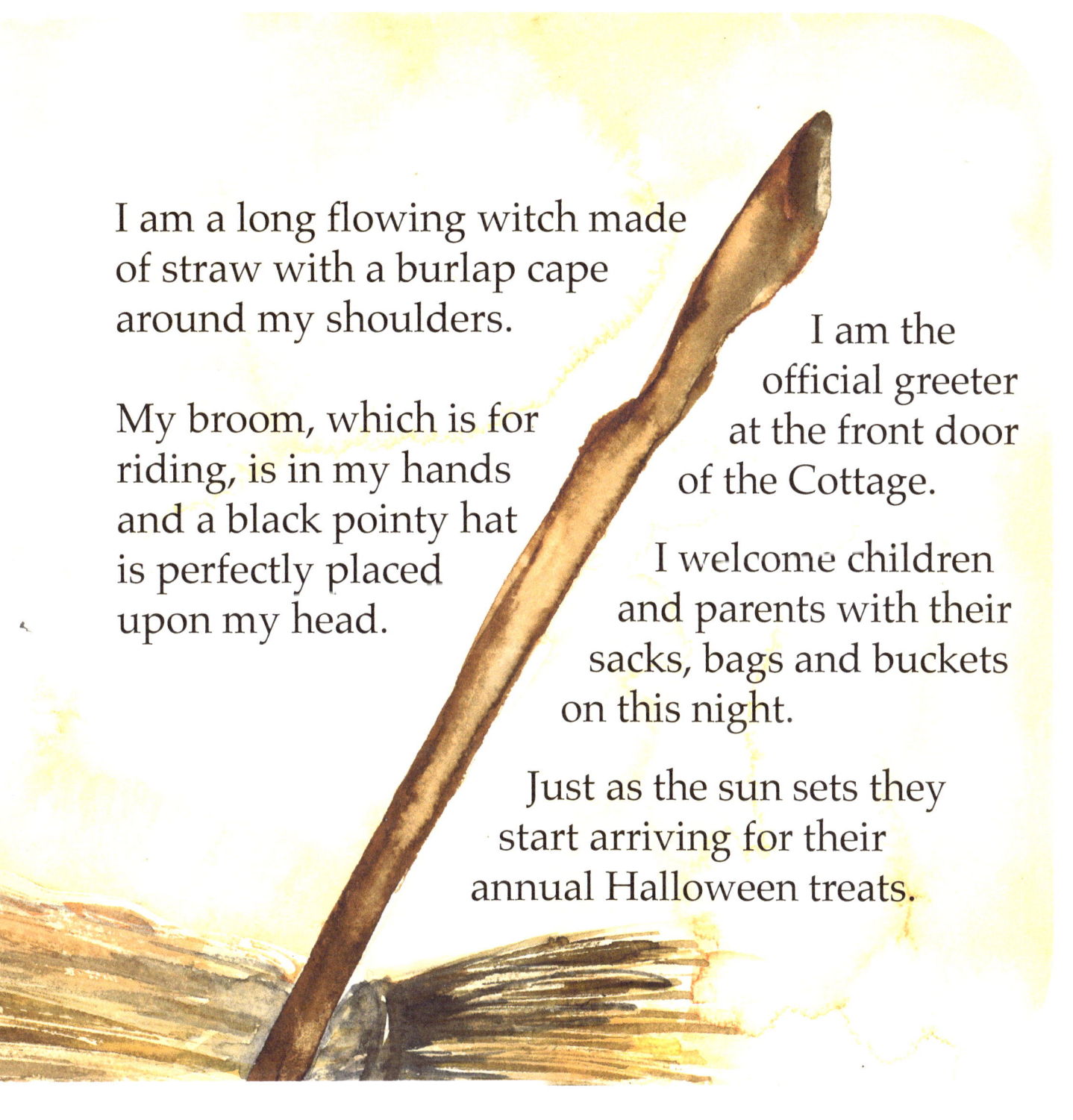

I am a long flowing witch made of straw with a burlap cape around my shoulders.

My broom, which is for riding, is in my hands and a black pointy hat is perfectly placed upon my head.

I am the official greeter at the front door of the Cottage.

I welcome children and parents with their sacks, bags and buckets on this night.

Just as the sun sets they start arriving for their annual Halloween treats.

They are on their way to our Cottage dressed in every costume one can imagine and their faces are often painted and one never knows what the hair may be doing! Some wear mask so it is very hard to tell who they are and sometimes they don't say a word so their voice won't give them away. They do a great job with their disguises.

I know if the Cottage doesn't treat our visitors we all might be tricked so I am on my best behavior this very special night.

As the offical greeter on this night of Halloween,
October 31, I would like to share a story with you
before the sun sets and our guest begin to arrive.

You see, two days ago a mischievous creature played a trick on me and it was such an adventure I knew you would want to hear all about it.

And it is true, every bit of it.

Now for the story...

Two days before this special night the window washers came to clean away the summer dirt and spider webs so I was moved from my place at the door to a bench under two big trees.

Debbie, the mistress of the Cottage, had no idea what was going on around me while the windows were being cleaned; at least not until she returned that afternoon to take me back to my spot at the door.

"Wink, where is your black pointy hat?" Debbie asked. It was no where to be found, not next to me, not under the bench, and not under the bushes around the trees.

I knew where it was and we had a problem. I had to have my hat; no self respecting witch could welcome in Halloween without a proper hat.

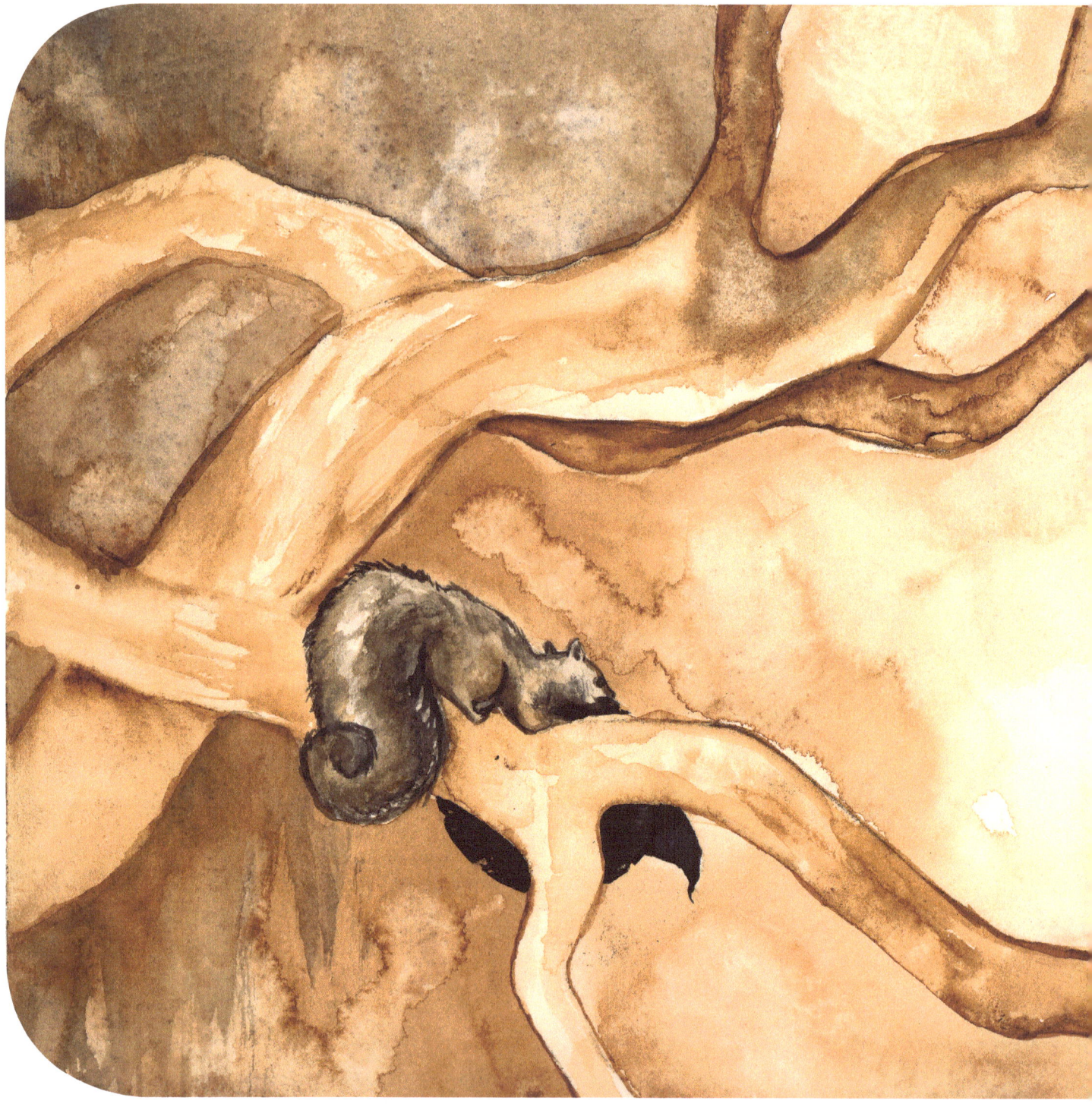

As Debbie looked around for the hat, she didn't know it but a gray squirrel with a big fluffy tail was watching her from above. He had told me his name was Gabby and when his chatter started, she looked up and saw him sitting on a branch of a big tree with my black pointy hat in one of his paws!

"*You took Wink's hat,*" Debbie said to Gabby. Holding the hat in his paws and looking down at us, he began biting on the tip and brim of my hat.

Debbie tried to shake the tree so the hat would fall but the tree was too big to shake.

I felt powerless without my hat so all I could do was sit on the bench and hope Gabby would come to his senses!

He was having a grand time, jumping around the limbs and scampering up and down the tree trunk and chewing on my hat. He did this for several hours and as the sun began to set he headed for his nest high in a tree across the yard.

"Please leave the hat behind," Debbie pleaded as Gabby jumped from limb to limb.

He ignored the pleas and when he reached his nest he and my hat disappeared for the night.

I sat all through the night thinking, *"I'm going to keep my eye on Gabby's nest and hope he doesn't decide my hat looks better in his nest than on my head. Oh, I will probably never see it again. What am I going to do?"*

It was a very long night and just as I thought I couldn't stare at the nest any longer the sun began to peek through the trees and I saw something move around Gabby's nest. Then I saw him and he still had my hat!

At the same time, Debbie came out to see if maybe the hat had fallen from the nest during the night. Then she saw Gabby sitting on a tree branch just like the day before, holding and biting my hat. I thought, *"He loves my hat, what am I going to do?"*

I imagined him placing that hat on his head and even though he was making me mad I had to admit he was a very clever squirrel. Then I watched as he carefully placed it in the fork of the tree and then began searching for his breakfast. I thought, *"Maybe the wind will blow and the hat will fall while Gabby is having his breakfast. That would be lucky."*

At that moment Debbie began to toss small rocks towards the hat hoping to knock it free from the tree but it was just too high to reach and no wind was blowing to help us out. After hours of pleading with Gabby to return my hat Debbie said, *"Oh well, Wink, don't you worry, and I will go to every store in the neighborhood if I have to. You will have a hat for Halloween."*

In all the excitement, I had forgotten tomorrow was the big day. It wasn't going to be easy to find a hat just the right size and shape for me. *"Oh well,"* I thought, *"my job is to keep watch on Gabby and wait patiently for a miracle."*

I began day dreaming about my new hat. *"What will it look like? Will it be a different color, shorter, taller? How will the brim be, wide or tiny? ...wait, what is that noise? Oh no, I was day dreaming and have lost sight of Gabby. Where is he? That noise... it is that silly Gabby chattering away again! I wish he would stop chattering so much. What is going on? Oh my, he is scampering towards me with my hat in his mouth!"*

In the mean time, Debbie was going from store to store looking for the perfect new hat for me. So far, either the store had sold out of witch hats or the ones they had were too big or too small. On the way back to her car she was passing by one last store, and there, stuck in a dusty corner of the window, was the perfect hat. She rushed in, bought it and hurried home to show me what she had found.

Meanwhile, Gabby stopped scampering in my direction and sat near the bench looking up at me. He took the hat from his mouth and chattered his chatter and then, placing the hat back in his mouth he jumped on the bench right next to me. I looked at my hat and other than a few bite marks it looked great. He looked around me, sniffed around me and just like the day before he began to climb my body. I felt him touching my cheek, then my head.

"Wink, Wink, I found a perfect hat," Debbie was saying as she ran towards me. As she got closer she suddenly stopped. She couldn't believe her eyes. The sight? Yep, you guessed it... there on top of my head was my hat, the one Gabby had taken! Gabby was on his way back down my body just as Debbie stopped in her tracks, her mouth hanging open, speechless and amazed, looking from my black pointy hat to Gabby and back to me.

Everything was very quiet and still. Gabby sat next to me for a minute gazing adoringly at the hat. His little paws that had carried my hat all over the yard were sweetly folded at his chest, his little mouth that had been so full of chatter and the hat was silent. Then he turned as if with a shrug and scampered away.

So that is the story, the trick that was played on me before Halloween. Along with the trick I was given a very big treat. I have to wonder, did Gabby grow tired of the black pointy hat? Did he love the hat but decided it would be the right thing to return it to me?

What do you think?

Debbie

Debbie Rankin resides in Marietta, Georgia with husband Ed and two Korat cats, Sadie and Churchill. She is a lover of nature and her home sits among gardens where wildlife abounds. The birds and other animals have very busy lives full of endless examples of the humor and challenges of life.

The Cottage in the Park is the affectionate name for Debbie and Ed's home and the land upon which it sits which are inspirational in every way. From the birds, to the critters, to the plants and minerals, she is reminded every day that all of creation has life. Everything has a past, present and future full of love, laughter, challenges and pure beauty.

Born in Virginia, Debbie has lived throughout the South. She spent over twenty years in the corporate world which included owning and running a successful consulting firm before focusing on other interests.

Although Debbie paints and writes about many things, in 2009 the focus became publishing her long overdue series of children's stories, all written many years ago. Butch the Blue Jay launched the series and now Debbie is proud to present The Squirrel Who Almost Stole Halloween. All stories are based on true events, and this fun story was written 10 years ago.

Please visit *www.cottageinthepark.com* for information about the series, and join the Cottage journey along with some of Debbie's favorite animal characters she has been privileged to know.

Kelly

Kelly McKernan currently lives in Marietta, Georgia. She is a graduate of Kennesaw State University where she received her Bachelor of Fine Arts with a concentration in drawing and painting.

In the spring of 2008, Kelly decided to pursue a career in illustration and set out to create a portfolio of work showcasing her talents. While doing so, she quickly garnered attention as a promising emerging artist. It was not Kelly's expectation to succeed as a fine artist as well as an illustrator, however. In the time since, she has been able to do just that. Kelly has shown with many notable galleries, been published in a number of major publications, and has received strong recognition locally, nationally, and worldwide.

The Squirrel Who Almost Stole Halloween is Kelly's second book with Debbie's Cottage In The Park series. Her weapon of choice is watercolor, but she also combines film photography with alternative printing processes into her paintings.

Aside from painting, Kelly has a background in working with children as a caretaker and a teacher with various art programs. She feels that the enthusiasm that rises from working with children is a form of inspiration in itself, as they view the world so simply and appreciate the seemingly smallest of wonders.

In Kelly's free time, she enjoys watching films, riding her bike, baking cupcakes, and contributing to furthering Atlanta's art community.

Eastern Gray Squirrel Facts

People who live in the suburbs will tell you squirrels can really get on their last good nerve! Squirrels think it makes perfect sense to live in your attic like one of the family, or chew big holes in your favorite bird house because it looks like a great place to live. I can get so irritated with them I want to scream. But when it is all said and done, they are like all of God's creatures, with good and bad sides, just like humans. They can be funny, very clever, sweet, charming. They can also be the biggest brats you would ever want to meet and a boundary is not a notion that comes easy to their very innovative brains.

Latin name is Sciurus carolinensis. The Carolinas is where the species was first recorded and remains very common. Now they are common throughout the eastern and southeastern states, some midwestern states, up and down the California coast plus portions of British Columbia. It is also found in Britain, Italy and South Africa.

Description; in the southeast the fur is predominantly gray with shades of brownish-red around face, shoulders, back and tale. The underside is white and some have what I call a thin black mustache. The males, especially as they mature, will display from time to time a very masculine posture with a stiff broad walk. It is most noticeable when establishing territorial boundaries.

The colors of the Eastern Gray Squirrel vary as they spread to other regions of North America and world.

The nest is known as a den. Generally built in forks of trees, they also favor tree dens, which are hollow trunks of trees. They will nest in large bird houses mounted on trees intended for owls and woodpeckers. Dens are lined with soft material like moss, thistledown, dried grass and feathers. In trees the outer den consists of limbs, sticks and dry leaves. *One year we had a very large den in one of our front yard trees. I noticed it had lots of sticks with green leaves which seemed odd. That is until I realized the squirrel was breaking fresh limbs from one of our azalea bushes. It was indeed one of the fanciest dens I have ever seen.*

Reproduction occurs twice a year, in the southern regions, December to February and May to June. The gestation period is 44 days and generally there are 2 to 6 babies in each litter. At birth they have no fur and cannot see. In 7 weeks they are weaned and 3 weeks later they leave the nest.

Adults average 9.1" to 11.8" in body length and the tale adds 7.5" to 9.8". Body weight varies from 14.2 ounces to 1lb, 5.16 ounces.

Communication skills are good and impossible not to notice when they are in a talkative mood! Their chatter is most common when a predator is around and a throaty sound most noticeable when they are annoyed with another squirrel. They also have a very sad cry which I have come to believe occurs when one may be injured or a friend has disappeared.

Their Eating Habits; they are hoarders with multiple locations for their stashes. They bury one nut or one seed, etc. in a spot under leaves or in the dirt, often very close to where they found the food, and return within hours to remove and place it in a more secure location. They have a remarkably accurate memory for distant and nearby landmarks to locate these stashes, and their ability to smell comes into play when they are within inches of the spot.

Food; tree bark, a variety of seeds, acorns, walnuts and other types of nuts and some fungi found in forests. Squirrels who live in sub-divisions demonstrate to us daily just how clever they are when it comes to their dining experiences! They keep the bird food stores in business with their unique ability to raid the most challenging of bird feeders. Driven by their seemingly bottomless tummies, they will study any challenge, even feeders hanging from wires, and will often win the battle.

Very rarely when their usual foods are scarce, they will prey upon insects, frogs, small rodents including other squirrels, small birds, their eggs and young. They will also eat bones.

Predators; include humans, hawks, skunks, raccoons, domestic and feral cats, snakes, owls and dogs.

(special thanks to Wikipedia for providing the image and some valuable facts)

www.ingramcontent.com/pod-product-compliance
Lightning Source LLC
Chambersburg PA
CBHW041522280526
45792CB00004B/1350